Part of the Five Little Dumplings Book Series:
Five Superhero Dumplings Champions of Kindness
Five Little Dumplings Get Ready for School
Five Little Dumplings The Lunar New Year Feast
Five Little Dumplings The Real Easter Story
Five Little Dumplings The Real Christmas Story
Five Little Dumplings Christmas is Almost Here
Number Tracing Practice Workbook Five Little Dumplings
Alphabet Tracing Practice Workbook Five Little Dumplings
Reading Comprehension Dumplings Five Superhero Dumplings

Jeremiah 29:11

Five Ninja Dumplings
ABC's
Kelsey Chen

A

A
is for
apple.

B

is for a

bear

with a

balloon.

Cc

c
is for a
cat on a
cloud.

D

D d

is for

ninja

dumpling.

E

E e

is for

elephant.

F
is for
f fox.

Gg

G
is for
giraffe.

H

h

H
is for
horse.

I i is for

ice cream.

Ice Cream
Ice Cream

Jj

J
is for
jellyfish.

Kk

k is for koala.

L l

is for

lion.

Mm

M
is for
monkey.

Nn

N
is for a
nice
narwhal.

O o

o

is for

orange.

Pp

P

is for

panda.

Qq

Q

is for
quail.

Rr

R
is for
rabbit.

S s

s
is for

sheep.

T

T
is for
tiger.

Uu

U
is for
unicorn.

Vv

V is for **volcano**.

W
w

W
is for a
whale in
the water.

X x

X is for xylophone.

Y
y
Y
is for
yogurt.

Zz

z is for zebra.

A B C D
E F G H
I J K L
M N O P

Q R S T

U V W

X Y Z